Sleep Tight

Grace Hallworth

Illustrated by Lisa Kopper

CAMBRIDGE
UNIVERSITY PRESS

"Close your eyes and go to sleep."
Mum kissed Lesley Ann
and turned out the light.

Lesley Ann shut her eyes tight, tight,
and counted sheep
the way Dad taught her.

One sheep and two,
how do you do?

Three sheep and four,
come to my door.

Five sheep and six,
I'll teach you some tricks.

Seven sheep and eight,
walk through the gate.

Nine sheep and ten,
into the pen.

But Lesley Ann couldn't sleep.

She heard the bull-frogs at the creek
crying, "Okio, okio, okio!"

Snug in their nests,
baby birds chirruped softly,
"Chereep, chereep, chereep."

But Lesley Ann couldn't sleep.

Crickets chirped, and fruit bats
in the mango tree shrieked,
"EEK, EEK, EEK!"

So Lesley Ann couldn't sleep.

Night filled her room with
darkness and shadow shapes.

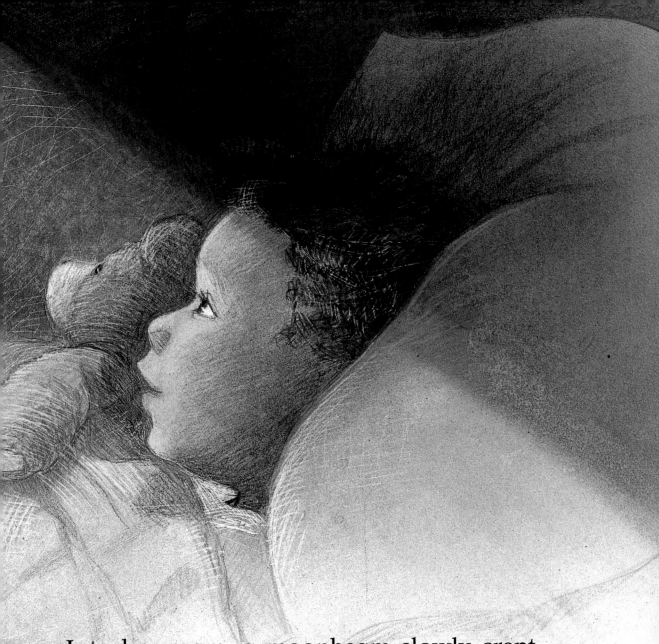

Into her room, a moonbeam slowly crept
until it reached her pillow.
"Hello!" it said,
and its smile lit up her face.

Gusts of wind slipped through the shutters,
played around her face,
gently brushed her cheeks,

and whispered,
"Goodnight,
sleep tight."

And Lesley Ann fell asleep.